An Earth Full of Gratitude

An Earth Full of Gratitude

A Collection of Poems

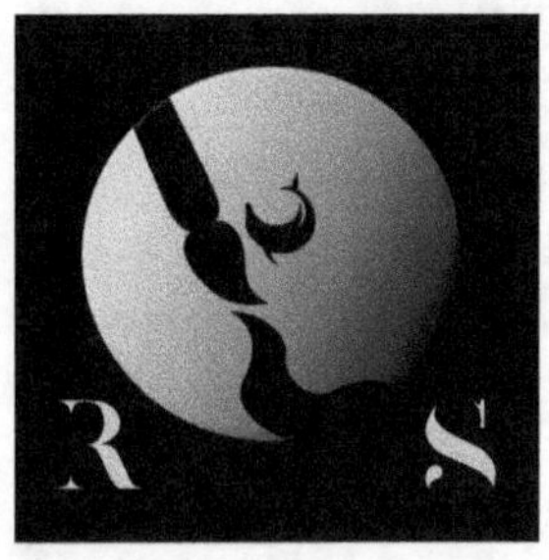

RANJITH SIVARAMAN

Foreword by Melissa Korber

Introduction by K. Genesis

RESOURCE *Publications* · Eugene, Oregon

AN EARTH FULL OF GRATITUDE
A Collection of Poems

Resource Publications
An Imprint of Wipf and Stock Publishers
199 W. 8th Ave., Suite 3
Eugene, OR 97401

www.wipfandstock.com

PAPERBACK ISBN: 979-8-3852-7435-2
HARDCOVER ISBN: 979-8-3852-7436-9
EBOOK ISBN: 979-8-3852-7437-6

VERSION NUMBER 03/17/26

Dedicated to
My Beloved. . .

"If you loved someone,
You loved him, and when you
Had nothing else to give,
You still gave him love."

—George Orwell, *1984* (1949)

Contents

Contents

Permissions

1. Eulophia (https://terrorhousemag.com/eulophia/)—Originally Published in Terror House Press Magazine (which is based in Budapest, Hungary), on 18th December 2020
2. The spring of Her Love (https://terrorhousemag.com/eulophia/)
   Originally Published in Terror House Press (which is based in Budapest, Hungary) Magazine on 18th December 2020
3. The Shortest Distance (https://www.sadgirlsclublit.com/post/the-shortest-distance-ranjith-sivaraman)
   Originally Published in Sadgirlslit (Literary Magazine of Sad Girls Club, which is based in New York, USA) on 24th September 2020.
   This poem was also featured on LKMNDS podcast (Produced in Partnership with The Elevation Review& Kneeland Centre for Poetry Inc, Indiana, USA) on 10th November 2020
   https://radiopublic.com/the-lkmnds-podcast-W024B4/s1!c4909
4. Bar tailed godwit—Originally Published in Adelaide Literary Magazine No. 44, which is based in New York (US), and Lisbon (Portugal) on 9th January 2021.
   https://adelaidemagazine.org/2021/01/09/bar-tailed-godwit-by-ranjith-sivaraman/
5. The Angel and the Dirty Kid—Originally Published in 'The Inside Brilliance' magazine and featured in the 'Havik Awards and Publication Ceremony' organized by the prestigious 'Las Positas College' California, on 8th May 2021.
6. Men, Why do you love me, Your Tender Lap, & Moonlight Goosebumps—Originally published in 'The Parliamentary Literary Journal, based in New Jersey on 16th May 2021.
7. The Seventh Spring—Originally published in The Silver Birch Press, Los Angeles on 2nd June 2021.
   https://silverbirchpress.wordpress.com/2021/06/02/the-seventh-spring-by-ranjith-sivaraman-i-am-still-waiting-series/
8. You Burned Us Day and Night—Originally published in poetrysndcovid.com, on 8th June 2021. It is a project funded by the UK Arts and

Humanities Research Counsel, University of Plymouth, and Nottingham Trent University.
https://poetryandcovid.com/2021/06/08/you-burned-us-day-and-night/

9. There is Someone—Originally published in poetrywivenhoe.com based in Essex ,UK on 29th June 2021.
10. The Pillow—Originally published in 'The Writer's Club' , Uk on 17th July 2021.
https://greythoughts.info/clubpieces/the-pillow
11. Coffee Bean—Originally Published in the August 2021 edition of 'Writer's and Reader's Magazine' ,UK and Litterateur RW Magazine, India
12. I Have You Only—Originally Published in the 'Wordcity Journal, Albertta,Canada on 19th September 2021. Also Published in the October 2021 issue of 'The Raven Review' Texas.
https://wordcitylit.ca/2021/09/19/i-have-you-only-a-poem-by-ranjith-sivaraman/
https://www.theravenreview.org/i-have-you-only-sivaraman.html
13. Three Dots—Originally published in the 'Three Moon Magazine' based in the unceded territory of the T'kemlúps te Secwépemc.
14. Unsolved Problem—Featured in the Queer Toronto Literary Magazine, website Canada, on 12th November 2021.
https://qtmag.ca/gallery/4IRQYFMOr7ccpwT80PSKuU
15. Cloak of Solitude, Sonnet to SPB, & Secluded Silences—Originally published in 'The Modern Literature' Magazine published from Chennai, India on 12th November 2021.
https://www.modernliterature.org/poems-by-ranjith-sivaraman/
16. My Grande Dame—Originally appeared in the *How to Heal the Earth* poetry series by The Silver Birch Press, Los Angeles in November 2021.
17. 'I know it'—featured in the 'Intangience Magazine' published from the USA, in June 2023.
18. On Those Moments—Published in 'Deep Over Stock Magazine' Portland, Oregon, USA, in July 2023.
19. Aid from the above—Published in Querencia Press, LLC, Chicago, USA, in June 2024
20. Moments without You—Published in Stanford University's Poetry Journal—Mantis.in Summer 2023 edition.
21. Heart of Parijat—Published in The Garland Magazine, Melbourne, Australia in their December 2023 edition.
22. I Accept—Published in Panorama Magazine, UK, in April 2024
23. 'Forgiveness—Published in Orenaug Mountain Poetry Journal', Connecticut, USA, in July 2025.
24. I Hide You—Published in The Zest of the Lemon', a literature magazine, from USA, in June 2025
25. An Ocean of our own—Published in The TV-63 Magazine, Middletown, USA, in October 2025.

26. What we dreamed of—Published in Ivo Review, Oklahoma, USA in December 2025.
27. The Waits worth our Lives—Published in Autumn 2025 issue of *The Bleeding Margin*

Foreword

In 2021, in those fragile days as the global pandemic declined, a poet on the other side of the world from me cast a fragile tendril across the distance. He sent a poem to the students I advise in California.

That poem, "The Angel and the Dirty Boy," won the approval of the discerning student editors of *Havik, the Las Positas College Journal of Arts and Literature.* It was published in the 2021 edition of the book, *Inside Brilliance,* one of many strands that collectively reflected on a journey that that found solace in the kinship created by art and the endurance of love.

That poet, Ranjith Sivaraman, worked his way into our consciousness then with a love poem based in reality, self-acceptance, and adventures born from dreams.

Now, years later, in a less hopeful world, but certainly one even more desperate for the quiet and contemplative spaces Sivaraman creates in his poetry, *An Earth Full of Gratitude* emerges. In it, Sivaraman showcases his work, including "The Angel and the Dirty Boy," guiding readers through strands that contemplate love and life from all angles, managing both tragedy and togetherness, heartbreak and longing, creating a lovely trellis from the tendrils.

Sivarman's voice is both dreamy and grounded in *An Earth Full of Gratitude,* transporting its reader in time, space, and faith to a quiet place where love can survive and grow even when faced with the cruelty of the modern world.

Enjoy your journey, readers. I anticipate that you will return from it as I did, with gratitude.

Melissa Korber
Journalism and Media Studies Faculty and Program Coordinator
Advisor to The Express, *Naked Magazine*, and *Havik*

Acknowledgment

Sincere gratitude to all poetry editors
who believed in me and accepted my poems.

Introduction

"Hidden from leaves, clouds
Sunshine, Moon, stars
Flower and Thorns
I have a deep root of wisdom
And an earth full of gratitude,
To keep me going,
Wherever love carries me along."

An Earth Full of Gratitude does not open like a book; it opens like a heart that has learned how to wait and how being in love feels. The book opens like a benediction: This is not showy devotion; it is *rooted devotion.* The root—wisdom—has been shaped by both petals and thorns. Gratitude becomes the ground, a Sufi earth where the heart practices presence. To read these lines is to feel steadiness: even in longing, there is a sacred steadiness that keeps the ordinary world habitable.

Having lived with these poems over time—returning to them through journals, pauses, and quiet rereading—I have come to understand that this collection is not written from urgency, but from blessing. It belongs to a man whose life is shaped by structure and responsibility, by calculation and caution, and who therefore approaches love the way he approaches truth- slowly, carefully, and with reverence. The voice here is not eager to impress. It is eager to remain.

Reading *An Earth Full of Gratitude* by Ranjith Sivaraman is like entering a soft dusk where moonlight and incense meet—an intimacy that wants to be felt before it is named. I am a woman who studies the social science and how love shapes bodies, choices, and speech. I hear the disciple's hush beneath devotion in this collection, I can imagine his beloved's face before the last line of his poems, I am in search of the imprints for a love that refuses the transactionality of our times. Here, The author of this book, is an engineer by habit and a simple businessman by life—measured, careful, always rehearsing the next step—yet his heart learns the audacity of surrender. He falls slowly, with caution, and then he falls utterly.

Reading this collection as a female, an Urdu poet and a Social scientist, *I feel the research-spectrum come alive as living seasons* (especially the autumn and spring in this book).

> *"And the sky became a garden of roses,*
> *Some pink, some red but without thorns. . . (I Sit Hoping)*
> *A purple flow with a tint of pink,*
> *A musk rose fragrant honey,*
> *A long wild strumming of guitar,*
> *What else she can say. . . (On Those Moments)*
>
> *"a wet thorn red deep inside*
> *and while you lie bleeding*
> *you can feel her walking away*
> *with a smile, after placing*
> *a pink wreath on your chest." (Pink Wreath).*
> Oh it's brutal. . .

The poems capture infatuation as combustible hunger—

> "My *Heart Becomes A Dandelion*
> *Forgets Everything and just floats*
> *I Love You and My Heart Whispers,*
> *'You Are Mine'" (My Heart Becomes A Dandelion)*

A dizzy, dopamine-bright plunge where the masculine howl and the feminine moon, first meet in urgent longing; they render attachment as tender domestic gravity—

> *"Of each night in a smile and gifts me,*
> *While sunshine wakes me up from your hug."*
> *(An Earth Full of Gratitude)*
>
> *"beneath the layers of his love*
> *The hugs of all strengths" (The Pillow)*
>
> *"you keep on hugging me where my love sprouts"*
> *(You Keep Hugging Me. . .)*

—the oxytocin hush of breakfasts, names, and quiet belonging.

The book's voice then learns the language of choice and steadiness: lines like

> *"When my quaver meets*
> *a premature death in my throat. . . I have you only"*
> *(I have you only)*

transform obsession into a deliberate pledge, the psychological secure-bond. Commitment appears not as duty but as heroic tenderness.

> *"Like the calm sea assimilating a fresh river*
> *I stood cold looking into her deep eyes.*
> *Even the Neelakurinji seldom knows*
> *The path of spring and blooms in 12 years of blue." (The Shortest Distance)*

—repairing, staying, forging roots beneath storms—while soulful love ascends into Sufi light: *ishq* that dissolves ego, *fana* that refines, *sabr* and *tawakkul* that turn longing into gratitude.

Ranjith's feminine imagery—craving, moon, mist, tender lap—meets male desire—wolf, howl, hunger, strength, determination—not to reduce love to bodies, but to show how *eros and eros's restraint* braid into devotion; where science maps neurotransmitters, *this book maps the soul's circuitry.* I find this relatable to the Modern scholars and thinkers like *De Amore* by Andreas

Capellanus, who agreed to the courtly love (fin'amor) was not about marriage, domesticity, or even sexual fulfilment. On the other hand, psychologists often read courtly love as an *early articulation of limerence*, but with spiritual discipline that leads to the Sufi shades in this book.

As we study, *emotional mechanics:*

- Obsession without consummation
- Heightened attention and sensitivity
- Idealization rather than realism
- Pain as proof of sincerity

This maps onto:

- **Attachment theory** (anxious longing)
- **Flow states** (poetry as emotional regulation)
- **Sublimation** (sexual energy redirected into art)

Love in this collection often arrives as a hush: a mist, a tide, a howl that belongs to the moon.

> *"If you want to know*
> *Why a wolf howls at full moon*
> *Fall in true love."*

Here the animal cry is not feral rage but *the language of longing—an old, mythic correspondence between masculine howl and lunar light.* The beloved is the moon; the lover, the wolf. In Sufi terms, this is *fanaa*—the dissolving of the lover into the Beloved—followed by the tender return, *baqā, of a remade self.*

Some lines make me think of a walk in mist holding hands and hugging near river banks under moonlight, the festival of love lit by diyas and the hush after fireworks of not lust but deep and spiritual surrender:

> *"She smiled at me as full moon*
> *Touched me as monsoon rain*
> *Hugged me as mountain mist."*

These images are sensorial *prayers*—rain on skin, the naughty nectar fragrance of a hornbill, mist that cools the brow, the sea that receives the sunset. They are also social images: a man who takes his responsibilities seriously learns to love without spectacle, finding in small rituals (a cuppa, a folded letter, a steady hand) his way to the divine.

The speaker's shyness turns poetry into sacrament.

"She was the unheard melody
Who made me a Poet."

I personally feel that LOVE is A *discipline of feeling to explore*, not a physical act.

In short: this collection is an elegy and a laboratory both—where pain and joy are braided, and the final finding is as beautiful and simple as true love, where everything else grows quiet like his "Wild Flower."

He cannot always say what he feels; he writes it. The poem becomes the body-language of the heart—quavers, sighs, goose bumps noted and treasured. In "I Have You Only" the voice confesses its refuge:

"When my quaver meets a premature death in my throat
. . . I have you only."
This is attachment as sanctuary: when speech dies, another presence carries the meaning.
Pain and pride coexist in pink—the color the poet returns to like a beloved's shawl.

In "Pink Wreath" the wound is tender and ceremonial:

"while you lie bleeding
you can feel her walking away
with a smile, after placing
a pink wreath on your chest."

The image reads as both grief and benediction: the wreath is an act of love that does not erase pain but honors it. The Sufi readers can feel the paradox—love that heals by naming the hurt.

Though emerging in different geographies, scholars often note striking parallels.

Jalal ad-Din Rumi (slightly later, but philosophically aligned) describes love as:

- Separation (*firāq*)
- Burning
- Longing without possession
- Ego dissolution
- Creativity through pain

> *"I know you are the lonely moon*
> *and I am the only wolf,*
> *and I know my howl will echo*
> *endlessly in your eternal moonlight."*
> *(Why do you love me?)*

The collection is full of small, sacred gestures—waiting like a festival's final lamp, listening like waves that accept the river, smelling wild flowers in a crowded market. In "I Sit Hoping,"

> "*Moon became another Silver rose,*
> *not hiding her thorns.*
> *I set my love free as clouds*
> *And the sky became a garden of roses."*

Even the poet's courage is tender and distressed: boldness lives beside helplessness; responsibility sits with heightened sensitivity. He is at once the man who builds and the man who weeps—brave enough to remain, humble enough to surrender.

Reading these poems through a sociological lens, I see devotion practiced as discipline: hope becomes prayer, waiting becomes worship, surrender becomes blessing. The poet's gratitude is social as well as spiritual—he offers us a loving economy in which care, faithfulness, and attention are worth more than conquest or cleverness. For a world thick with facades, these pages offer a soft insistence that true love—patient, pink, demanding, forgiving—still takes root.

From a psychological lens, this is where love transforms behavior. The poems register small bodily truths: waiting without agitation, noticing expression before speech, sensing emotion before it is spoken. The poet reads the beloved not through words, but through presence. Her love—honest, steady, almost divine in its constancy—gives him permission to feel fully. Because she loves him so deeply, he learns to trust his own sensitivity. And yet, he remains shy. Speech doesn't express his vast love for his beloved, his muse. So he writes. It is said that the "Poetry is the breath and finer spirit of all knowledge" (William Wordsworth's *Preface to Lyrical Ballads*).

His poem "Scent of Milk" deserves an in-depth analysis, especially for the current and future generations to preserve and cherish.

SCENT OF MILK

Any fresh day when she sees me
there is a smiling moon floating
in her deep calm eyes.
A full moon, jumping out from the dark clouds
like the dancing dolphin of Arabian sea
like the sensation of hearing
a soothing voice for the first time,
like the Goosebumps erupted
on the back of neck on first kiss,
like the gasp of fresh air

like an adorable baby
who still expects her mom to feed her
long after the breasts forgot the scent of milk.

Well, I was confused between the "Scent of Milk" and "Pink Wreath" although both the poems equip the reader to travel into different but extreme emotions. In a single sentence, I find the "Pink Wreath" bleeds whereas "Scent of Milk" *breathes.*

As a woman reading this poem from the core of soulful love, I experience it not as desire reaching outward, but as love *circling inward*, which is rare and is the best skill of the poet i.e. translating emotions, *toward origin*, memory, and *the most ancient. . .innocent form of intimacy* the human psyche knows.

This poem strikes because it does something rare: it dissolves romance with childhood and save true love to *instinct.*

It hits so deeply. . .

As the title suggest, Milk is the *first language of the body.*

Any fresh day when she sees me
there is a smiling moon floating
in her deep calm eyes.

Before words. . .Before choice. . .Before longing becomes desire. It is love. . . pure love! We fall in love without choice without words, only heart knows where it belongs. The language of silence and feelings. Similarly, He look at her with same intensity. His heart falls, when she meets him with a vibrant moonlit smile and devoted sight.

A full moon, jumping out from the dark clouds
like the dancing dolphin of Arabian sea

The depiction of full moon jumping out from dark cloud could be the blinking of her shy eyes or the glimpse of her bosom that dance like dolphins.

like the sensation of hearing
a soothing voice for the first time,

He might be analyzing the sensory difference in her voice with different pitch when she feels love intensely.

like the Goosebumps erupted
on the back of neck on first kiss,
like the gasp of fresh air

That very change of her sight and voice gives him goosebumps and the intimate sensation like a cold wind blowing and kissing at the back of his neck.

like an adorable baby
who still expects her mom to feed her
long after the breasts forgot the scent of milk.

Psychologically, scent is the strongest trigger of memory—processed not by logic but by the limbic system, where attachment, safety, and emotion live. When the poet chooses *milk*, he is not speaking of erotic love, He is touching the *pre-sexual, pre-ego bond*—the place where love means belonging, survival, nourishment, being held without asking. He might be recalling the sense of security and devotion in Love.

As a female reader, this lands in the womb-space of emotion, because the Milk carries:

- maternal warmth, unconditional giving
- honesty, search, destination
- softness without negotiation
- love that does not demand to be returned
- belonging and devotion

This is not love that wants you.

This is love that *keeps you alive.*

The poem begins where attachment begins, in scent, skin, breath, memory.

Before masculinity performs strength.

Before femininity performs beauty.

The feminine energy in this poem is not eroticized, it is *elemental.* She is nourishment, earth, cow, breast, morning, kitchen, silence. She gives without spectacle.

For the masculine psyche, this is disarming.

Male desire usually moves outward—toward conquest, intensity, expression. But here, male consciousness is *humbled.* That realization is pain of past and soothing at once.

This is love that chooses reverence over ownership.

From a research lens, this is secure attachment at its most refined, the ability to feel closeness without panic, warmth without control.

From a Sufi lens, this is *return—ishq* turning back toward source.

Best lessons: There is no promise spoken aloud in "Scent of Milk." Yet commitment is everywhere. Commitment here is not about staying with a person, but about staying *tender* in a harsh world. The poem commits to softness and devotion.

And then it crosses into *soulful love*:

Milk becomes metaphor.

Scent becomes prayer.

Memory becomes gratitude.

This is love without demand.

Love without future bargaining.

Love without fear of loss—because it has already been given.

Soulful love, in this poem, is not transcendence upward. It is transcendence *inward.*

IN ONE QUIET TRUTH

If "Pink Wreath" teaches us how love hurts beautifully, "Scent of Milk" teaches us why love heals silently.

It is the poem where masculinity rests its head. Where femininity becomes earth again.

Where psychology meets devotion. And that is why it persists . . . like a scent you cannot name but know has always been yours.

Ranjith depicts Poetry to become the space where love can be said without being announced. Again and again, the poems suggest that writing is not ambition, but necessity. She becomes the muse not because she inspires art, but because she makes feeling possible.

> *"She was the unheard melody*
> *Who made me a Poet." (Melody of her soul).*

Love does not decorate his life; it creates his language.

This collection understands love in the Sufi sense—not as possession, but as surrender. In "The Shortest Distance," closeness is not measured by proximity but by dissolution:

"drop by drop, cell by cell, breath by breath."

Love is not something one reaches; it is something one enters and is changed by. In "Us" and "I Never Left," love is defined by staying—not loudly, not heroically, but faithfully.

Nature moves through these poems as companion, not metaphor. Moon, autumn, leaves, rivers, dew—these are witnesses. In "If Love Is a Season Forever," autumn teaches how to remain together even as things fall away. In "Oh! Moon," the moon is shy, generous, retreating—much like love itself. The world here responds to emotion, as if recognizing it.

Grief, too, is part of this journey. But grief is never performative. In "Grief Is a Wisdom," sorrow teaches without declaring itself. In "Pink Wreath," heartbreak unfolds gently, painfully, with each attempt at healing revealing deeper tenderness. Pain is not denied; it is honored. Pride in love remains intact even when love hurts.

What moved me most, as a social scientist searching for traces of true love in a time of performative intimacy and emotional shortcuts, is the gratitude that holds this book together. Gratitude not for perfection, but for the chance to love at all. Gratitude for being changed. Gratitude for having one person who makes life intelligible.

This book does not explain love, it practices it.

It does not argue for devotion; it lives inside it.

And for that—for reminding us that such love still exists, quietly, faithfully, without spectacle. This book is *the emotional spectrum* that held us gently starting with:

- **Infatuation** expressing desire, hunger, intensity, illusion; then feeling
- **Attachment** to provide safety, comfort, and belonging, which leads to the
- **True Love** by Choice, with clarity and steadiness. It firmly expresses

- **Commitment** with responsibility, resilience and courage. Silently turning towards the
- **Soulful Love** providing Meaning with surrender, gratitude, transformation and transcendence.

I read this collection with heartfelt gratitude. Not as a judge, not as a theorist, but as a witness.

Science explains *how* love moves through the body and brain. Poetry explains *why* we bow to it.

True love is not the loudest feeling. It is the one that remains when everything else grows quiet.

I close this introduction with a simple thanks: for the moonlit courage, for the mist that teaches tenderness, for the wolf's honest howl and the lamp that will not go out.

This book does not explain devotion; it is devotion—an earthly, luminous practice, guide, contribution and gratitude to love.

K Genesis
2026

Prologue

"Why we 'Fall' in love?"
My Beloved asked.

"Because, when we truly love someone,
We make the greatest leap of faith."
I replied.

AN EARTH FULL OF GRATITUDE.

Cradled by these leaves

And those clouds

Smiling like a baby cutie

Our love skies a moon mint.

Darling dew carries the moon and stars

Of each night in a smile and gifts me,

While sunshine wakes me up from your hug.

Hidden from leaves, clouds

Sunshine, Moon, stars

Flower and Thorns

I have a deep root of wisdom

And an earth full of gratitude,

To keep me going,

Wherever love carries me along.

OH! MOON.

In the visible fathom of tides

As her locks become flowing clouds

Oh Moon! I can sense what you feel inside.

Let her cuddle fondly while you shy

And just let her give back your sky.

DARLING AUTUMN.

Darling Autumn came peeping

From the sky and stood smiling

I smiled back with eyes covering

And kept my lonely bench hiding

And walked back to our love, sighing

Before I could see a single leaf falling . . .

MOMENTS WITHOUT YOU.

Moments without you

Have cute little teeth,

And my heart still tender

My soul still wonders.

For every bite

A flower blooms,

A tear weeps

and Rolls down fragrant,

I taste and my sigh

Flies into an afar sky.

FOR SURE.

One day for sure,

Like a swirling maple leaf

I will fall with you into

The red and wild of Autumn.

One night for sure,

I Will Hold your hand

And will saunter together,

To the mellow moon of desire.

I NEVER LEFT.

Even though, sun sets somewhere

without a word, without a look

Daily leaves me, a sky full of inks.

May it be the night hiding

Or Day welcoming

Wake up with a blessing,

Let love keep you going,

And always remember this,

The best feeling in love is,

'I Never Left.'

I SIT HOPING.

Moon became another

Silver rose, not hiding her thorns.

I set my love free as clouds

And the sky became a garden of roses.

Some pink, some red but without thorns.

I sit hoping that, a drop of rain,

a handful of moonlight, a pat of breeze,

will bring me the fragrance.

I STILL HAVE SIGHS.

As I have all my love

In my eyes, she chose to hide,

Hid and sent silence to hunt

In my heart, where her love hides,

I lay like dead, and her love held breath

But in my days, I still have sighs . . .

IF LOVE IS A SEASON FOREVER.

If Love is a season forever

May it be Autumn,

Each day be a leaf,

And hugging each other

Let's see it fall in its yellow

And smile in a pale sorrow,

And remind us to be together more

Kiss more and love a little more.

IN THE END.

'In the End,

we all become stories,' they say.

But lucky are, they,

Who become poetry.

'In the End,

we are all alone' they say,

But lucky are they,

Who have someone

To be lonely with.

ONE DAY.

I may fall short of words one day,
My pen may start
laughing at me one day,
This distance and silence may
Perch on my soul and heart one day,
This Pride and Coldness may
Have the last laugh one day.

Even then my beloved,
my head will be
Held high in our love,
that made you my poetry . . .

ONE SKYFUL.

One skyful of hope

Sings to my mornings

To love who found my soul home,

And live up to the blessings she gave . . .

SMILING SUNNY DAY.

Dews and dew looking droplets

Smiled and wished me, ‘Good Morning.’

I smiled them back, with a thought

That, for every crying rainy night

There can be a smiling sunny day.

TONIGHT.

Tonight, Moon is

A pale silver floweret

In this deep blue solitude,

Fallen from the warmth of

our alluring pink sky.

US.

I love ‘ Us ‘ a little bit more

Than ‘I love you’,

Because that’s where Love exists,

Not in You, Not in Me,

Deep inside the togetherness,

Called ‘ Us.’

WILD CHERRY WITH WINGS.

Honey, Be the chill

on my nape

When this sweatdrop

elopes with wind

Be the last taste that

remains on my lips

After you start feeling

me all over you

Be all that, what keeps

this night in blush

And my Heart,

a wild cherry with wings.

YOU KEEP HUGGING ME.

You keep on hugging me

Where my love sprouts

Somewhere I can't touch

But can ache but can't sketch

Somewhere I feel a leaf swirling

But can't sense the breeze hissing

Somewhere, I carry the tears clouding

But can't show my eyes darling . . .

ALL DAY LONG.

All day long, my heart sinks deeper
And she looks younger,
Day by day, my love gets sweeter,
And she skips heartbeat,
Step by step, she comes closer
And I gaze as far as my eyes can see
Drop by drop, I feel her dews
And she melts as wet as the sun sets . . .

I JUST HAVE ANOTHER DAY.

Some days I don't see
Sun, Moon, and stars,
I just have another day
Marching above you and me,

I just have one more step
Closer to you, deeper in love

I just feel a dew falling on
A pink petal without any noise,

I just see a bird owning a blue sky
And nearing a Gulmohar tree
Long waiting with a shade of hope.

I KNOW IT.

I know it when I am heavy
For the holding hands

I know it when the sweat
is too early and uniform

I know it when the footsteps
convey the familiarity of corridors

I know it when I realize
The warmth in greetings

I know it when rage run
Into each pulling

And I know it when
I hear the screams of innocence.

Synopsis: Thoughts of one of those guns, brought by one of those kids, into one of those classrooms.

ON THOSE MOMENTS.

A purple flow with a tint of pink
A musk rose fragrant honey
A long wild strumming of guitar
What else she can say,
More than these
of those moments.

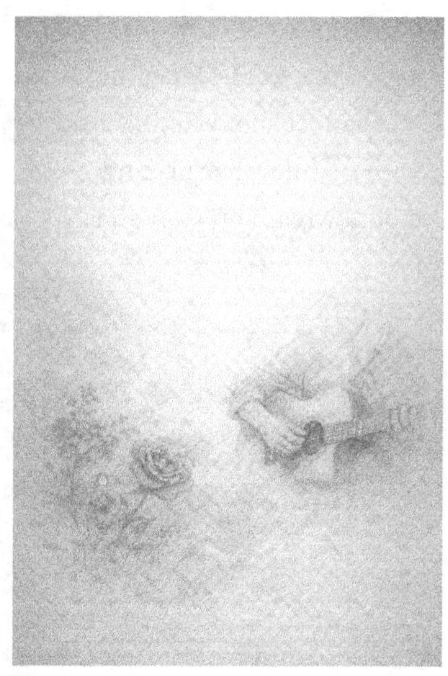

PINK WREATH.

When you are in love and sob
you feel the pull of a fresh stitch
Deep inside the wetness of heart
But all you can do is fake a smile
and try to fool the cry from another stab
and then a hiccup will come
with a wave of emotions
and you will sob again.
This time a stitch is meant
to be broken and broken red
then you will try to figure out
where you did wrong
and then then you can feel
a wet thorn red deep inside
and while you lie bleeding
you can feel her walking away
with a smile, after placing
a pink wreath on your chest.

WHEN I SIT LOST IN YOU.

When I take a deep breath, darling
A quaver smiles at me, hiding

When I sink in a sad melody
A sigh peeps at me, floating

When I get kissed by these cool breeze
A whisper tempts again me, passing

When I sit lost in you, darling
A day looks at me, hoping.

WHY THEY DON'T SPARE YOU.

'Why they spare You?'
They asked the Cow
"Because they think, I am mother."
Replied Cow.

"Why they spare You?"
They asked the Pig.

'Because they think I am disgusted.'
Replied the Pig.

Then both of them thanked Almighty for,
being born among the right men
and saving their lives from being cooked and served.

"Why they don't spare You?"
Then they asked the Woman.
'Because they think, I am disgusted and capable of being only mother.'
Replied the Woman.

Then three of them, thanked Almighty for keeping her still alive among men.

ONLY ONE SEASON.

'Goodbye' is a wild cherry on a hard Prunus
which has its roots entrapped in a cold Heart.
When someone gifts you that,
Your poor blooming heart can feel
a never ending Autumn.

When your heart was blooming
in the summer of Heliotropes
Her heart was having all seasons.
She knew the spring will come

And She knew the Cherry will ripe

She knew the leaves are born to fall
She knew the roots are strong to hold.
But she never knew that,
your summer was always fragrant
And in your Heart there was only one season.

SCENT OF MILK.

Any fresh day when she sees me
there is a smiling moon floating
in her deep calm eyes.
A full moon, jumping out from the dark clouds
like the dancing dolphin of Arabian sea
like the sensation of hearing
a soothing voice for the first time,
like the Goosebumps erupted
on the back of neck on first kiss,
like the gasp of fresh air
by a drowning damsel,
like an adorable baby
who still expects her mom to feed her
long after the breasts forgot the
scent of milk.

UNSOLVED PROBLEM.

I believe, we all have
one unsolved problem in life,
a dark forest where we are always lost.

For a few, that may be a secret
which hides like a grenade in the pocket

For a few that may be a maniac foe
who picked us just for fun

For a few, that may be the mediocrity
which dances on the tunes of our dear ones

For a few that may be the parental toxic Warfield
into which we helplessly personified

For a few, that may be the spring of a lifetime
in which we can bloom, but can't exude fragrance.

I HAVE YOU ONLY.

When my quaver meets
a premature death in my throat
When I curl up like a Chartreux
I have you only

When my eyes meet
a deep sea of darkness in my nights
When I see no face with warmth
I have you only

When my heart hangs
like a beehive on an abandoned mesquite tree
When I sink like an over ripe coffee cherry
I have you only

When my soul evaporates
into a fragrant cloud
When I rain like mistified drops
I have you only . . . .

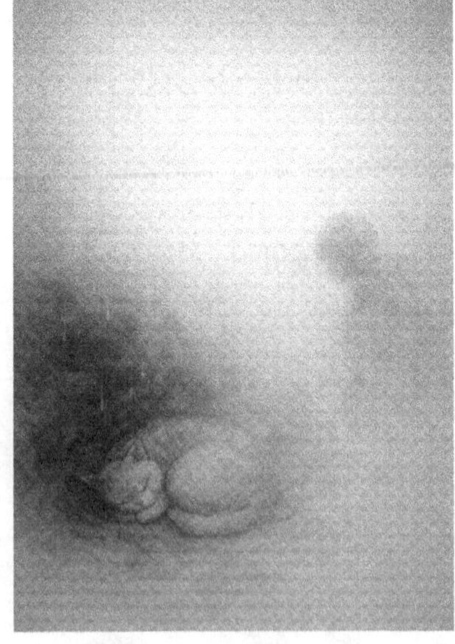

WHY DO YOU LOVE ME?

'Why do you love me?' he asked her.

'Because, you know how to love, what is love, and value love,
you need nothing other than love,

You dive into my eyes and breath freely in my heart,
You spill your soul into mine and I become you,

I always feel how precious I am and I preserve myself for you,
I always feel there is more love inside me for you,

you are that dew, where my sun becomes rainbow
you are that mist, where my tears grow feathers
you are that valley, where my fragrance solidifies into fruits.

I know you are the lonely moon and I am the only wolf,
and I know my howl will echo endlessly in your eternal moonlight.' she replied.

SOMETIMES.

Sometimes I see your eyes carry a baby
A baby with two dimples one large, one small

Sometimes I feel your lips make a curve,
A curve which hides a mine of Goosebumps

Sometimes you give me a smile,
A smile which tickles my soul with moonlight feathers

And then you give me expressions,
Those expressions for which I was dying my whole life.

EULOPHIA.

Life is a dual between promise and love
A dual with strange rules
Sometimes one opponent never enters
And even if enters, winning is irrelevant
But you are always on the losing side
You want both to win, which is near to impossible
In this strange dual, one opponent is always late
But this late entry makes all the difference
Your life is taken for a rollercoaster ride
Your heart becomes a velvet cake
And you lie stone-cold taking the cuts
You wish you could scream and run
But you are sinking into a bottomless ocean
You are blooming in an endless spring
Also falling as a pale yellow maple leaf
You are on the top of a snowy mountain
Also thirsty as a Eulophia in the cruel desert.

THE SPRING OF HER LOVE.

Love is an invaluable gift
Wrapped in insecurity
And opened with possessiveness.

When love melts into soul
A poem is born

If you want to know
Why a wolf howls at full moon
Fall in true love

She smiled at me as full moon
Touched me as monsoon rain
Hugged me as mountain mist
And trusted me as love of life

Every time she smiled at me
Autumn and spring bloomed in heart
Dawn and dusk melted down to sea
Life and death frozen in time

She found herself
In the depths of my love
I lost myself
In the melody of her soul

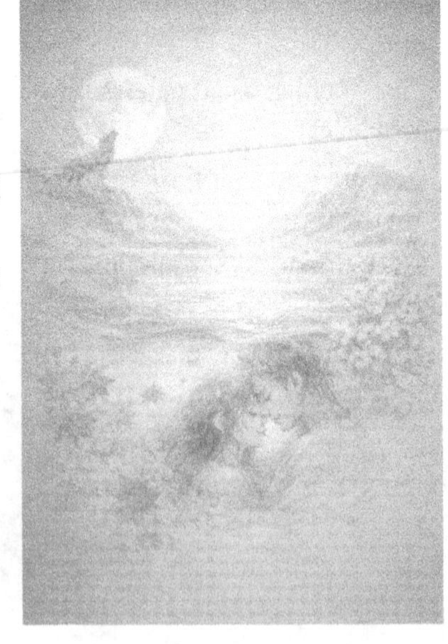

I kissed her shadow in my dream
I bloomed in the spring of her love

She was the unheard melody
Who made me a Poet

When touch is a mirage
Love craves, heart bleeds
And soul howls

The thin line drawn by helplessness
Decides the fate of the lives of lovers

I will keep you so happy, I told
Tears were rolling down her cheeks
At that moment in the west
Wounded sun was again disappearing
Into the calm sea.
When the poet in me dead
I knew she was the poem.

THE SHORTEST DISTANCE

'Which path has the shortest distance
To reach you?' my beloved asked.
Like the calm sea assimilating a fresh river
I stood cold looking into her deep eyes.
Even the Neelakurinji seldom knows
The path of spring and blooms in 12 years of blue.
Even the Hornbill seldom knows
The path of first raindrop and ends it's wait.
'Drop by drop, cell by cell, breath by breath
I was dissolving in you, melting into you.'
Tears were rolling down her cheeks.
At that moment in the west
Wounded sun was again disappearing
Into the calm sea.

*Neelakurinji—A flower which blooms once in twelve years can be seen on the hill ranges of Munnar in Idukki district of Kerala, India.

**Great Hornbill—Indian Grey Hornbill is symbolic with the endless wait for Rain, (A belief in the State of Kerala)

BAR-TAILED GODWIT.

'What happened?
You are lost in deep thoughts
Looks like you made a long solo trip
Like a bar-tailed godwit'
I asked my beloved.
She continued her meditating trance
Smiled, showing her soul,
And finally landed on earth.
'When we are silent
One part of my soul
And one part of your soul
Start a beautiful conversation
Holding our hands
They float, fly and migrate
Back in time, up in the constellation
Deep in bliss, lost in future
They keep on talking
When I am awake and asleep
When I cry, laugh, sigh
When I bleed, break, breathe
One part of my soul
And one part of your soul'

BACKBULBS.

Was she right about
The Snowy Mountain?
She thought, Moon covered it with silver
And morning Sun turned it into Gold.
Mountain reminded her, of her father
Tall and well built, who always stood for her.

Maybe she was right about
The waves and seashore too.
She thought, the sea calls her
By humming endless tunes and waving her foamy hands.
Sea reminded her, of her mother
Who kept her on the lap, kissing and caressing

'Have you seen the rising sun
Through the airplane bleed holes?
Floating on the clouds
Looking us eye to eye
Like the lover boy who lives next door.'

She taught me: to walk bare feet
On wet mud and get vibes,
To call the stream sweetie
After the feast of gooseberry
To play second fiddle to cuckoo
To read the letters from the moon to the tides
And to help the wild orchid to count her dying backbulbs
To cherish the nostalgic springs.

SONNET TO SPB.

You are the sweet mist in my labyrinth
The feast of gooseberry to sweet stream
The letter from the moon to Macbeth
The taste of blueberry with a wild scream

I, dream of a starry night;
Bloom in a Spring of Goosebumps
I feel autumn in my sober heart
And my sorrows fall as leaves

I cry and tears make me blind
I sigh and lips hold my breath
I lose in past as a hummingbird
And take the greatest leap of faith.

My ears deliquesce in a Celestial River
And ripples dance on my soul floor.

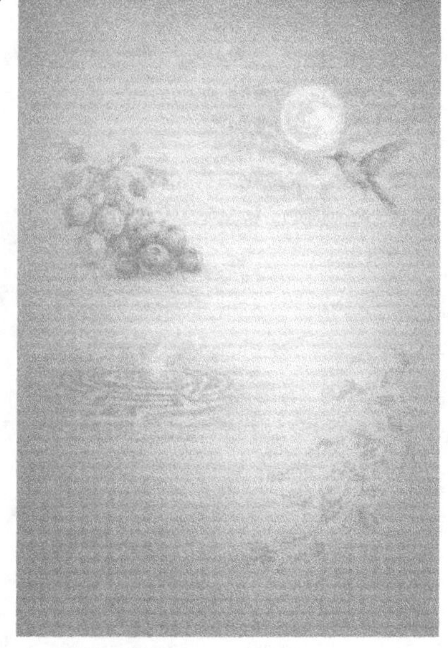

Synopsis of Poem 'Sonnet to SPB'

When we listen to our favorite singer or music, the emotions and transformations we go through are divine and magical. I am one of the passionate fans, of singer S.P.Balasubrahmanyam.

He went on creating ripples on my soul and my sonnet is born.

COFFEE BEAN.

Kabini* was carrying the coracle** and me
like a phlegmatic old man who carries a Palanquin
and I saw you floating towards me
sitting on a banyan tree leaf
covered in red thin skin and sweet pulp.
I never saw you this beautiful.
You were always cold and dark brown
like a meditating monk.
I always loved your heady scent
when you come to me
in a freshly brewed pot.
You awaken my spirit,
flavour my life,
and smell like soulful love

Coffee Bean, You are the one who taught me
to enhance the colour of each moment,
to refresh the aroma of each breath,
even if life puts us in boiling waters.

*Kabini—A river in India, originates in the Wayanad District of Kerala state.

**Coracle—A traditional round shaped boat.

THE ANGEL AND THE DIRTY KID.

The kid loved playing in the mud
A mud much darker than his skin.
He was comfortable being dirty and ugly
Because all his mates were so.

Deep inside him always dreamed in vain
of a cute little angel who will descent from the sky
with an alluring smile and tempting soul
The angel took his hand and slowly made him clean
They walked into the woods, climbed the hills
ran through the plains and swam in the rivers
they admired the orchids, pissed off cuckoos
drenched in sunlight and burned in rain
They tasted fragrances drank tears
danced in storm, fought for memories
hugged breathlessly and froze in moments

And kid asked the angel, 'where are your wings?'
The angel told him 'I forget to mention;
I was never an Angel, but I didn't want to hurt you with the truth!'

MEN.

Is he not aroused?
Why no fire of wild lust in his eyes?
Doesn't he realize the moments are dying one by one?
We both don't know when our breaths will dance together again.
Or is it only my heart is young?
His eyes found no feast
and keep looking stone cold.

He was very different and expert virtually
Like a wild beast tearing down the screen
I think I should leave,
run girl run, with what is left of your dignity.

He was missing an indistinct lullaby and kisses drenched in tears
the cutest scolding of elder sister
the naughtiest wrying of younger sister
he was not there to utilize the chance
he was in search of what he needed
and he was finding what he was missing all his life . . .

YOU BURNED US DAY AND NIGHT.

Are you a natural selection or invention?
If natural selection, I have nothing to say,
And if you are invented, let the 'splendor of thousands of suns,'
Blaze upon the heads of your inventors.
You took the touch, taste, smell, and smile
You changed human life forever.

The first was a wave and the second is a tsunami.
You made us walk hundreds of miles
And die on the road.
You denied us air, floated us dead in the river
And burned us day and night.

You made us fight for cylinders and states for vaccines.
You laughed at statues and other billions wasted in vain.
You made oxygen another tool for men to get women.
And yet in all these traumas

You treated every caste, creed, gender, and sect equally,
And You revealed our friends in need.
You let the true leaders and captains arise

And the fake ones get exposed.
You showed us the Gods and Angels,
Gods with stethoscope and Angels with the syringe.
And we still believe that,
"Even the darkest night will end and the Sun will rise."

THE SEVENTH SPRING.

I saw the dark pillars and boles
And my body was darker than normal.
Fire apples were hanging
from the leafless trees
and the breath tasted
like searing fragrance.

I was in this burning forest
as far as my evanescent mind flies.
The forest remembers everything,
the first raindrop that kissed me
and missed me forever,
the second cloud that rained over me
and stained me forever,
the third drizzle that danced with me
and replaced me forever,
the fourth lightning that struck me
and shocked me forever,
the fifth flood that drowned me
and crowned me forever,
the sixth river that washed me
and baptized me forever,

Then I saw a white little angel
holding her magic wand,
wearing, the cutest smile
and few ephemeral snowflakes.

She was an ethereal moon
set aflame in a tragic sky.

I know she is on the other side of the fumy river
But I am still waiting like a phoenix who outlived nine ravens.
And I know she is the seventh spring that will transform me
and dissolve in me forever . . . .

THE PILLOW:

I know all my mute dreams and memories
Are safely locked in your heart.
You even felt my secluded cries,

the silent sighs, and the most obstinate Roars.
O-My pillow, my dear pillow . . .
Thank you for being there for me
Thank you for listening my madness
Please don't tell anyone these secrets

I told you in this sleepless night . . . Do you have a bleeding heart of your own?
How can you feel my killing love?
The fragrance of night Jasmine makes me cry . . .

I can't stand outside.
Dear Pillow, Every time I miss my beloved,
You offer me your edges to get wet
With tears of my helpless grief
and tolerates my kisses silently
And returns me the warmth of his chest.

I miss those cuddles and smile,
The mild musk fragrance of his soul
The taste of chocolate mousse
beneath the layers of his love
The hugs of all strengths,

the faith in his eyes,
The need in his wraps,
when he made me feel like a fragrant mist.
Hey Dear Pillow . . . are you listening?

THREE DOTS . . .

Three dots . . . were left wounded
awaiting the 'inevitable sound of death.'

Till recently these three dots . . . were our lifeblood
Now see, the poor dots are bleeding to death.

The dot in the middle, melted two souls into one
and we were more than happy to be dots.

I remember the days we fought for these three dots . . .
'where are my three dots . . .', 'I need more three dots . . . '

But Darling, now these three dots . . . are left wounded
awaiting the 'inevitable sound of death.'

I know the first dot is me, my ego
and the third one is you, your ego
and of course the second one is 'Love'
and they say 'God is Love.'

THERE IS SOMEONE

There is someone to love me too
Such a love that made me love myself

There is someone who misses me
Such a miss that I started missing myself

There is someone who craves for me
Such a craving that I started feeling the pull

There is someone who transforms me
Such a transformation that I will live forever

There is someone who weeps for me
Such a weep that I feel the burns of tears

There is someone who trusts me
Such a trust that I am proud to be human

There is someone who made me a destination
Such a destination which feels home forever

CLOAK OF SOLITUDE.

When her eyes are blank and cold
When there are no ripples of warmth
When they are like a frozen brook in a new moon night
When they look at me still perceive no image
When the darling shy dews are missing
When I keep searching for the sparks of her soul
When her lips forget to make curves
When her smile hides in serious thoughts
When her love falls in a lonely meditation
My Heart again fights with me
My Mind again starts missing me
My Soul again wears the cloak of solitude.

GRIEF IS A WISDOM

Grief is the voice of
Silence creeping on distance.

It's the drop of hope from
A suddenly dimmed star above

It's the excuse of moon to not smile
Dream to not rise and sun to not wake you up

It's the wisdom that keeps you at door
Without ever disclosing, house is empty.

MY GRANDE DAME.

I never felt my legs since six,
And ever loved my lake since then
My boat was my cradle
And my lake was my Grande Dame.
I remember those greener days,
When my lake was pure
And my oar was free
from the floating bottles.
I never felt my legs since six
And ever loved my lake since then.
My boat became my last hope
And bottles became my close friends.
I saved them from my lake
And rowed them to shore
And they told me their story,
Poor fellows were born to be abandoned.

Synopsis of Poem:

This poem is dedicated to a poor old man (who is paralysed below his knees) collecting plastic waste from the Vembanad lake and other streams of Kumarakom, in Kerala, India.

He would hire a small country boat and venture out to collect plastic every day, early in the morning; he would manoeuvre using a stick or his oar. He mainly collects plastic bottles that were dumped in the waters.

YOUR TENDER LAP.

I was a nomad wandering
In the streets of love
Seeking a humble abode.
I delved the deserts,
Climbed the mountains,
Hunted the pearls
And slept fainted
On the river bank.

When woke up
The river was no more
But I found myself
Floating on your tender lap.

MOONLIGHT GOOSEBUMPS.

Honey,
Through the uneven emptiness
Of these dancing leaves of
Our favourite Kadamba tree,
rain out into me
as cloud soaked
Moonlight Goosebumps.

LAST WORDS OF AN AUTUMN LEAF.

The fallen Autumn leaf

Was on his last days

Supine and sighing.

' It's painful to be forgotten,

But I love this, even it's bed ridden.

Up there among them,

I was left out, to become forgotten.'

The tree smiled and just dropped

Another one to the credit of Autumn.

AID FROM ABOVE.

He was running on fire
With a greater fire inside

He was not aware of
The Mannah from Heaven
Or his name written on
The grain fell from Heaven

He was running on fire
With a greater fire inside
Hoping a grain of kindness
At least from the aid from above.

Synopsis

Five people were killed by an aid airdrop package when at least one parachute failed to properly deploy and a parcel fell on them.

There were two boys among the five people killed.

I ACCEPT . . .

While these long shadows of Sunset
Cast their spell to the youth of Night,
I look forward to the call of Moon
In Her Star-studded transparency,
I accept the Silence of Night
With its faintly hidden Meaning,
I accept the Surprise of Dreams
With their daintily woven Longings.

FORGIVENESS.

Forgive everyone who loved you
For not loving you as you need
And this may make many laugh
As they did no mistake really
And who you really are to
Give them forgiveness.
But, what they know about
What love has done to you
And How you loved.

I HIDE YOU.

The Day has its offerings
And the Night has its Silence,
Somewhere in the yearnings of twilight
I always felt your last touch of the day.

Again There will come seasons
And small and big reasons
We say 'I Love You' with a kiss
And I say, 'I Hide You in my blush . . . '

WHAT WE DREAMED OF.

When all those sunsets put together
I feel it looks like
the spring we dreamed of.
Wafting golden hues

above the tickling waves
Etching molten orange
along the horizon,
All look nothing short of
the flowers we dreamed of.
The extended glow of twilight
The impatient wait of night
All remind nothing but
that day we dreamed of . . .

WHATEVER COMES WITH LOVE.

Whatever comes with love
Let it come and the rest be gone
Whatever is not taken as love
Let it go and the rest be gifts
Whatever keeps one busy
Let it be normal and the rest be a surprise
Whatever is missed to be understood
Let it be so and the rest be clear
Whatever gifted as poetry
Let it be forever and rest be forgone.

MY HEART BECOMES A DANDELION

I Love You And
My Heart Becomes A Dandelion
Forgets Everything and just floats
I Love You and My Heart Whispers,
'You Are Mine' Believes that
and just dreams
I Love You and My Heart
Prays To Give More Strength
To Bear Everything
After the Dandelion lands
And the Dream ends.

I DREAM OF US.

My window loves the youth of night
My pillow loves the wait for daylight
Between these, I dream of us
And I usually extend it into my days
And that is my poetry . . .

AN OCEAN OF OUR OWN . . .

We all need an ocean of our own
that becomes a tender tide
and sees us as its moon,
that hides invaluable treasures
in the depths of its desire,
that becomes rain drops
just to dance wet with us
that keeps coming back to
our shore for a reason
that makes it feel like home.

THE SPACE BETWEEN THE STARS.

I love the infinite space
Between the stars of this sky
Which tells me I am yours
Being caressed by the twinkles
And showered by the moonlight
Sometimes hidden by
the whiteness of the clouds
And sometimes by
the blindness of my eyes.
Yet, I love the infinite space
Between the stars of this sky
Which reminds me
She is my infinity in love.

SIMPLY.

I am so curious when you appear
Like the first rain arrives in the courtyard
Like the nearing mist dews my windshield
I simply get wet in rain
I simply inhale more and more mist
I simply get lost in the feeling of you
I simply get lost in the feeling of love . . .

I WILL TELL YOU WHAT I CALL IT.

Wish I could glitter with
The spark in your eyes,
Wish I could curl into
The smile on your cheeks,

Wish I could be the dew
I tasted between your lips,
Wish I could be in everything
That becomes your
craving for me.

There is something in
Both of us, that
Keeps us away
And keeps us together.
What keeps us together
is what matters to me,
And I call it, ' Love . . . '

THE WAITS WORTH OUR LIVES.

Near the heaps of flour sacks
Hunger discovered that
Our waits can be worth our lives.

Even when realizing that
What is ground and mixed
to make up for the shortage,
is not something meant
to be fed to humans,
We acknowledge that
Names worth our lives
Are written on each grain.

It is true that,
Silent creatures
Always congregated
around the feed provided,
yet even they had
the luxury of time
to appease their hunger.

When blood splattered
on the wheat flour,
when bullets tore through
tiny, starved bellies,
those who wove white shrouds
to cover 'survival' ceremonially,
named it, "Flour Massacre."

SOME SPACES

Like the deserted encroachments
Once made own, then left on itself
We all have some spaces in our hearts
That never really crave footsteps of love

Like the cobwebbed corners of a forest shrine
Only cleaned on the auspicious day
We all have some spaces in our hearts
That never really mind distance or silence.